Seiji

Seiji An Intimate Portrait of Seiji Ozawa

PHOTOGRAPHS BY Lincoln Russell

EDITED BY Caroline Smedvig

INTRODUCTION BY John Williams

HOUGHTON MIFFLIN COMPANY · BOSTON · NEW YORK 1998

Compilation and text copyright © 1998 by the Boston Symphony Orchestra
Photographs copyright © 1998 by Lincoln Russell
Introduction copyright © 1998 by John Williams

For information about permission to reproduce selections
from this book, write to Permissions, Houghton Mifflin Company,
215 Park Avenue South, New York, New York 10003.

Library of Congress Cataloging-in-Publication Data is available.
ISBN 0-395-93943-7

Printed in the United States of America

Book design by Robert Overholtzer

STN 10 9 8 7 6 5 4 3 2 1

Contents

Preface

It was Indian summer, October 1979, when I was first presented to Seiji ("Maestro Ozawa to you," sniffed an officious aide-de-camp). Mortified, I retreated to a corner to await my turn; as if I would have ever dared *tutoyer* on the first audience. The green room of Symphony Hall was strange and exotic terrain for a twenty-something writer, suddenly self-conscious about her reporter's uniform of cowboy boots and faded velvet jeans. I was finally motioned forward by then Assistant Manager Peter Gelb for my formal introduction. Emerging from a private inner dressing room in what I mistook for a kimono (only women wear *them,* I would learn), Seiji Ozawa wiped his still dripping wet jet-black mane, stuck out a hand, and, upon hearing my name was Kim, pronounced, "Funny, you don't look Korean."

Lincoln Russell's arrival on the scene was, coincidentally, simultaneous with my own, and I think probably just as daunting. From our first assignment together to chronicle a BSO load-out to Carnegie Hall, we have teamed up in the ensuing twenty years for a total of twelve tours to Europe, Japan, and of course numerous assignments back at the ranch at Symphony Hall and Tanglewood. We no longer think it unusual that Seiji greets well-wishers in a custom-made cotton robe we now know as a *yukata,* embellished with the

kanji for "Seiji." The green room, with its ebb and flow of the elegant and eccentric, is familiar turf, home plate, as is backstage, onstage, offstage, and clearly—judging from many of the photographs—après-stage.

But the one aspect of this life which is never routine or commonplace is Seiji himself. I remember something Leonard Bernstein said at a late-night party following a Tanglewood concert in which Seiji had conducted some impossible program, all from memory. Lenny pounced on Seiji, grabbed his face between his hands, and exclaimed, "What planet do you come from?" Many of the tributes that appear here grapple with this question, as all of us who know Seiji inevitably try to explain his hold on us.

Seiji is utterly without pretension or self-importance—unusual in a milieu where those attributes are often cultivated, if not required. A year ago in Paris, following a performance Seiji conducted, a seventieth birthday celebration for his dear friend Slava Rostropovich, we went together to a soirée at the French White House, the Élysée Palace. Arriving late and further delayed by his frantic curbside necktie tying, we both realized that neither of us had brought the invitation card to present to the phalanx of guards dressed in Napoleonic military splendor, complete with bayonets. Seiji approached the one in charge, grinned, and pulled out the lining of his pants pockets to demonstrate our faux pas. In no time, we were banished to the service entrance. Seiji cheerfully complied, and as we made our way across the courtyard, France's First Lady, Madame Chirac, spotted his retreat and dashed to the rescue. The sea parted. At the table, he was the life of the party, regaling the king of Spain, Princess Caroline, and Prince Charles with counsel on when to split tens in blackjack, along with other indispensable advice. Yet their celebrity didn't seem to register with him. "Nice party" was his sincere and only comment on the evening.

But woe to anyone who mistakes his breezy nonchalance and self-effacing manner for a casual approach to his work. In fact, the very worst thing I have ever heard Seiji level at anyone—and it was indeed meant as a severe criticism—was "He is not serious." As Lincoln's photographs taken on the podium attest, Seiji is as intense and relentless and serious about music as is humanly possible.

Over the past two decades, I have felt at times like a Sancho Panza, a water boy, a consigliere, a colleague. When Seiji's daughter, Seira, writes so movingly in her tribute of her father's possession of *jingi,* the Japanese word for loyalty in its purest form, it rings true and it runs both ways. He would fight to the death for what and for whom he believes in; he is generous in the extreme, defiant of convention and convenience, yet profoundly conservative when something is worth conserving. Lincoln and I have witnessed him within the grandest context and the most intimate, from the larger-than-life moments on the stages of Berlin, Salzburg, Tokyo, and New York to the smallest space—an empty dressing room, alone and unreachable.

To respond to Lenny's question, we can say that Seiji must be of this earth. Perhaps the best explanation of his prodigious and unique talent comes from his longtime manager and friend, Ronald Wilford, who has said: "Seiji is a humanist. He is a man who loves people, understands people, and is of the people." And never, ever, for a moment is he capable of being anything other than himself. That is, above all, what we hope this book conveys.

—CAROLINE SMEDVIG

Foreword

On a late Thursday night in November 1971, six trustees of the Boston Symphony Orchestra and its manager, Thomas Perry, secretly met with the thirty-four-year-old Seiji Ozawa in the exclusive wine room under the Amalfi restaurant next door to Symphony Hall. In a festive mood, they gathered to celebrate Ozawa's appointment as the next music director. The room was often the scene of postconcert cast parties, but this evening marked the beginning of an extraordinary quarter-century tenure that continues today. Within a few weeks of that meeting the secret was out. And in 1973, Seiji ascended the podium as music director for the first time.

Twenty-five years later, the Boston Symphony Orchestra is at the pinnacle of its artistry—carried there by a musical genius respected throughout the world. Most of the BSO players today are Seiji's appointees, so it is truly his orchestra. But as he always says, this orchestra has a heritage. The orchestral sounds are passed from one generation of players to the next. One hears the music of Beethoven or Brahms as if from a German orchestra—or a French orchestra when Ravel or Berlioz is performed. Seiji nods his head in wonder when he hears the music played in front of him. His ears perceive the influences of Serge Koussevitzky, Charles Munch, or Erich Leinsdorf, as well as the earlier conductors of the BSO. In some unfathomable way, he says, the older players pass it on to younger players, and the result is incredible. The sound of the BSO inspires awe and reverence. The credit has to go to this humble man. He has insisted on excellence and has the patience, moral strength, and work ethic, plus an amazing power of concentration, which enables him to get the best from himself and the musicians.

In the pages that follow, you'll read about the sensitivities, the humility, the determination, and the artistry that Seiji brings to his work. His fabled memory as a conductor is a gift. But, as he says, it takes work. Those who know him are aware of the immense time, the hard lonely hours, he spends in hotel rooms, preparing for a performance.

As he works hard, so he plays hard. Try beating him at tennis. He is as quick as a cat. Or watch him ski. He's always in control, even on the brink of disaster, as he was when he led the youth slalom in Nagano, Japan, this winter, on icy slopes that took him to the very edges of the restraining nets. His love of ordinary people is immense. At those Winter Olympics he taught several hundred of his "mountain people" from the surrounding highlands to sing Beethoven's "Ode to Joy" with the orchestra on international television, simultaneously with choruses from five continents. There is also Seiji sitting with his son, Yuki, watching the Boston Red Sox lose the third game in a row and the playoff series to the Cleveland Indians on a biting-cold October night, wrapped in a ski parka but staying until the last bitter out. Senator Kennedy once pulled strings to move up Seiji's jet to the head of a line of more than two hundred corporate planes waiting to leave New Orleans after the Super Bowl so that Seiji could get to Symphony Hall on time. (It almost worked.) Watch Ozawa conduct the fiftieth-anniversary concert of Britten's *Peter Grimes* and you'll wonder how, from memory, anyone can lead two different casts of the Tanglewood student orchestra in six memorable performances from a score that contains multiple rhythm changes, many from one measure to the next, and features fourteen soloists and a chorus. Or watch Ozawa take the BSO to Europe and play Mahler's Third and Sixth symphonies in London, Paris, and Vienna and receive such acclaim that he and the players take six curtain calls and finally leave the stage as the crowd continues to applaud.

His humility is matched by an overwhelming strength of character and honesty. Seiji never backs away from discord in matters of artistry. He can be conciliatory after taking a strong stand, but is never afraid of difficult challenges.

Now he is looking forward to his twenty-sixth year with the BSO, the longest tenure of any conductor in the orchestra's history. He seems to be working harder than ever, driven to build on the excellence he has achieved. In his mind the BSO can play the music of any era and any composer with energy and artistry and brilliance. Nothing is beyond his players, as visiting conductors are quick to point out.

At programming meetings he tries to preserve the difficult balance of the older, favored, and familiar repertory with contemporary compositions. He seeks established soloists, yet he never fails to support promising younger artists. But finally what concerns him is what is best for the BSO. He is generous with guest conductors, giving them the option of playing the most popular repertory, and generous also with acclaimed soloists. He reserves for himself the more challenging and lesser-known works, both old and new.

Those who work with him see this generosity and brilliance every day. They love him. This book captures that man.

—NICHOLAS T. ZERVAS
President
Boston Symphony Orchestra

Introduction

John Kenneth Galbraith, a wise societal observer, once commented to me that he was surprised at how much hard work was involved in a musical life and that he had thought only farmers worked really hard. I reminded him of the composer's writing cramp, the violinist's tender elbow, the conductor's aching back, and the singer's sore throat, not to mention their frequently exhausting travel schedules. These difficulties are all familiar, but no bona fide musician would ever trade them for a more comfortable lifestyle. After all, the performance of music has a unique place in the tapestry of human experience. At the fundamental level of nonverbal communication, it functions clearly as a defining human element, and although we don't entirely understand *how* it works, we do know that music belongs to that "oneness" that unifies cultures. Whatever our language, we all know and "speak" music. Indeed, a few gifted individuals have also devoted their lives to interpreting the language and literature of music for the rest of us. Seiji has been one of those chosen few.

A life dedicated to making music is one of those rare human activities that can be both intellectually stimulating and physically invigorating. There is no better recipe for a productive and joyous life, and this book celebrates in photographs one of the most compelling illustrations we have of the life of a great, hardworking artist and a fascinating man: Seiji Ozawa.

Seiji's early history is singular and rare. Born to Japanese parents in China, he grew up in Japan, torn apart by a tragic war, in a family that was not particularly musical. Though his father was Buddhist, his mother was a Christian who introduced him to hymns on Sunday. (His first Western music in church: "What a Friend I Have in Jesus.") He was clearly one of those fortunate beings who seem to have been born with a mission, with that inexplicable but certain knowledge of why they are here. Seiji was then, as he is now, lit by a very bright inner light.

As a boy, Seiji, his father, and his brother loaded a small piano on a wheelbarrow and pushed it fifty miles to their home so that Seiji could begin his studies. To me, this story forms a powerful image of Seiji's innate drive and desire. Although his talent quickly made him a prodigy who caught the eyes and ears of Japan's best teachers, it was, fortuitously, a rugby injury that turned his gifts toward conducting. When he was a little older, he loaded a Subaru motorbike that he'd won in a music competition aboard a freighter and went alone, first to Messina and then to France, to continue his studies in Paris. Without financial help or a powerful mentor, he was driven not by raw ambition but by a sense of mission and vocation that has always animated him. A joyful, unstoppable optimist had begun the great adventure that would take him, in a few short years, from obscurity to the world stage.

His first great strike of good fortune—hard-earned as it was—came in the rather obscure French town of Besançon, where he won a major conducting prize. One of the judges happened to be an eminent conductor named Charles Munch who invited him to attend the Berkshire Music Center. It was through connections made there that Seiji came to the attention of Leonard Bernstein in Berlin, becoming his assistant at the New York Philharmonic. At the same time, he had the unbelievable luck to win over Herbert von Karajan, who would become his other great mentor beside Hideo Saito in Japan and Lenny.

From Seiji's earliest arrival in Lenox, Massachusetts, the young conductor must have been immediately identified as someone exceptional. He was then, as always, the possessor of a dynamic and powerful source of energy, a student from a distant culture, speaking no English, but one determined to study, explore, and absorb all that he could in order to fulfill his destiny and to make his own personal contribution to the world of music.

His prodigious memory immediately became apparent and must have been something truly astounding to witness. Seiji could then, as now, conduct the most detailed and complex scores without the aid of any sheet music. Indeed, he has told me many times that he finds it very difficult to conduct when he has not memorized the score. He feels the use of music impairs his eye contact with the players and that the need to turn pages restricts the use of his left hand, which is otherwise free to express and interpret. A spectacular example of this extraordinary gift occurred in 1983, when Seiji conducted entirely from memory the world premiere of Messiaen's opera *St. Francis of Assisi,* a huge nine-hundred-page tome of almost unfathomable complexity and more than five hours in length. He carried it off without ever giving the slightest hint of a mistake or miscalculation. Seiji's

aptitude for the art of conducting is consistently expressed at the genius level.

His professional résumé reads like a glistening saga of successes, including the directorship of the Toronto Symphony, the San Francisco Symphony, the Chicago Symphony's Ravinia summer festival, and finally his beloved Boston Symphony Orchestra, now twenty-five rich and rewarding years ago! His dedication to his orchestra has been unique in its constancy and commitment, and he is now celebrating one of the longest tenures in the history of orchestral conducting. By the richness of his interpretations and the power of his communicative skills, Seiji has given us countless ennobling moments and has, as Leonard Bernstein described it, been the caretaker of "dreams to be realized, responsibilities to be shouldered, standards to be guarded."

In rising to the challenges of this mandate, Seiji has compiled an impressive list of achievements. Particularly noteworthy, I think, are his countless performances of contemporary music, many of which have been BSO commissions. This year alone he has conducted the world premiere of Leon Kirchner's *Of Things Exactly as They Are* and Henri Dutilleux's symphony *The Shadows of Time,* both to rave reviews at home and on his recent European tour with the Boston Symphony.

From a composer's point of view, there are two types of conductors: the first will offer less than what your "inner ear" imagined the music to be, and the second will infuse the music with a beauty that is beyond what you have imagined.

Clearly, Seiji belongs to the much smaller second group. I had the rare experience of being in the audience when Seiji conducted my score from *E.T.: The Extra-Terrestrial*. As you might imagine, I have conducted this music in public probably five hundred times, yet I felt at that moment that it was different. Naturally, I wondered why. The notes were the same, but somehow Seiji's reach surprised me. He had rehearsed the piece very carefully, as though it had never been played before, and he seemed to find textures lying deeply within it which I had not realized. He seemed to be adding his own voice to the music, and it was as refreshing as it was revealing.

A perfect example of Seiji's sense of adventure was his performance of Beethoven's "Ode to Joy" for the opening of the 1998 Olympics in Nagano, Japan, in which he synchronized, by satellite, choruses from five continents. Watching Seiji then was a revelation. I had conducted the opening Olympic ceremonies in Los Angeles in 1984 and again in Atlanta in 1996, and I had loved it. The experience was wonderful, but I found it hard and difficult work. For Seiji the experience was filled with fun, joy, and a national pride that I both envied and admired. It wasn't enough that he conducted the orchestra for the ceremonies, but he also appeared on TV as the first downhill skier to salute the mountain, cut the ribbon, and declare the games open! His ebullience and *joie de vivre* illuminated the entire event and what must have been one of the single greatest moments of his public life.

Seiji's joyful spirit is also reflected in his private life. His radiant family is represented in these pages. Seiji was fiercely proud of his wife Vera's recent designs of the dancers' costumes for the opening Olympic ceremonies. He revels in the accomplishments of his beautiful and talented children, Seira, now twenty-six, and Yukiyoshi, twenty-four, who live principally in Japan after Seiji made what he calls "the hardest decision of my life": to have them grow up and study in Japan so they could fully assimilate to their culture.

Seiji, of course, has an army of friends, some of whom occupy very high places: prime ministers, artists, and celebrities of all sorts, as one might expect. However, this is not the whole story. His closest friends are without doubt those made early in life, long before any fame was established, and he is fiercely loyal to them.

Once, after a concert in San Francisco, Seiji invited a group of prominent local supporters of the orchestra, the composer Sir Peter Maxwell Davies, and a few other distinguished guests to a small supper party. The rather elegantly dressed group filed to their cars, some chauffeur-driven, and followed Seiji to the unnamed restaurant he had chosen. I remember being more than a little stunned when he led us into an empty nightclub for the late dinner and a private performance by a woman named Carol Doda. Surgically enhanced, she was the proprietress and star attraction at this place, which I later learned was a kind of mecca for the art of the striptease. Ms. Doda, I was told, was world famous and one of Seiji's oldest friends. She and Seiji greeted each other like a brother and sister after a long separation.

As the lights dimmed she began her dance before our dumbstruck little group in furs and dinner jackets. The tempo quickened and the audience, backlit from the stage, formed a picture that I'll never forget. Their eyes widened and their jaws dropped as they gazed in wonderment. I also caught a glimpse of Seiji. He was beaming.

This book reminds us in photographs that while Seiji is fabulous to listen to, he is also wonderful to watch. People say that his movements sculpt the music in a three-dimensional way. He is equipped for conducting in every physical aspect of the art, combining balletic grace with perfect balance and a precisely measured use of the available space around him. Seiji forms the ideal interpretive link among the orchestra, the music itself, and the audience. His gestures describe what we hear, carrying the music off the printed page, through the instrumental re-creation of the notes, sending it through the air shaped, balanced, and alive.

Seiji is arguably our most dazzlingly visual conductor. Purists will assert that music, being the quintessential art form, ought to be sufficient unto itself. Certainly there is much truth in this position. However, for many people in the audience, watching an orchestra bow, breathe, and move together adds greatly to the experience of the music and helps to explain why a recording can never completely capture the spirit of a live performance. In Ozawa's case, he's as rewarding

to see as to hear, and his unique physical gifts make him an obvious subject for a photographic chronicle such as this book.

There is certainly some accuracy in the cliché that one picture speaks a thousand words. After all, words often need translation, and their meanings and nuances constantly shift, never quite capturing the moment as precisely as a great photograph can. A photographer can preserve the essence of his subject and the subject's world in a way that no memoirist or biographer can ever duplicate. He can provide the historian with source material unmatched by any other medium. Imagine the treasures we might have had if a photographer could have captured, say, Beethoven composing at his piano or conducting in a concert hall. That is why this book is such an important contribution. Both Lincoln Russell and Kim Smedvig have been close friends of Seiji's for many years. A wonderful artist in his own right, Lincoln has recorded the kind of photographic history that can only be achieved by a portraitist who enjoys intimate access to his subject.

In this volume you will get a glimpse of a man who is exhilarated by his art and by every moment that he practices it. You'll discover his animation, vibrancy, and joy, for he is among those most fortunate of God's creatures who are nourished and sustained by the love of what they do.

—JOHN WILLIAMS

Conducting in Symphony Hall. Boston, 1979.

Back in the seventies, in the prehistoric, pre-cable days of television when PBS loomed like a rare and exotic landscape, I somehow stumbled on one of its Boston broadcasts. It was called *Evening at Symphony,* an elegant offering of weekly concerts by the Boston Symphony—not the usual musical fare that might have captivated a young filmmaker. But it captivated me. And that was not because of Schubert or Prokofiev or even Mahler, all of whom were wonderful discoveries in their own right. It was because of this fabulous creature on the podium—this lithe, balletic athlete with a shock of thick black hair and beads on his white turtleneck. It was Seiji Ozawa, whose energy and grace and dynamism completely entranced me. I never thought that our paths would cross, but it has been my great good fortune that through my dear friend John Williams I have come to know Seiji. What is perhaps most astounding is that his enormous physical gift is matched by his humanity. He is funny and kind. And I'm grateful to him for broadening my appreciation of the larger body of literature that comprises our musical inheritance.

—STEVEN SPIELBERG

Rehearsing in the
Teatro Colón.
Buenos Aires, 1992.

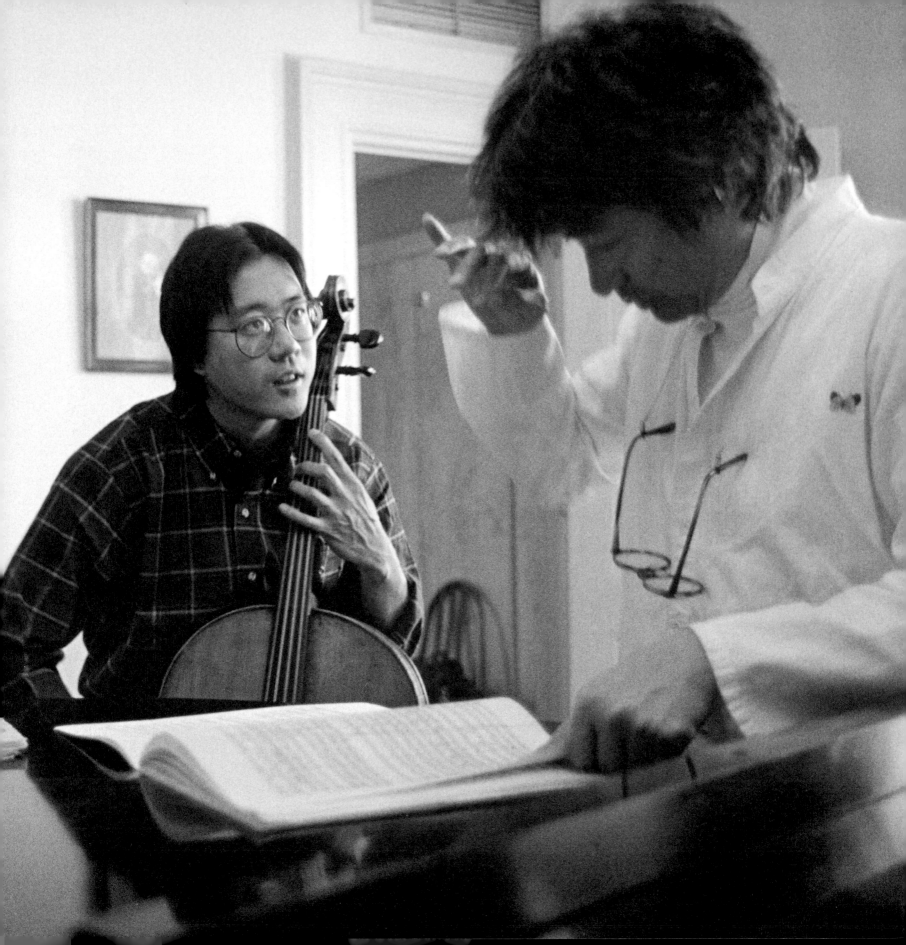

Backstage in the Shed at Tanglewood with Evgeny Kissin. Lenox, Massachusetts, 1993.

In the green room at Symphony Hall
with Yo-Yo Ma. Boston, 1988.

Rehearsing in the Grosses Festspielhaus, with Albert Maysles filming. Salzburg, 1984.

I feel very grateful to know Seiji Ozawa. We have been friends for a long time and we've often played music together—many works, with many different orchestras.

Playing with Seiji is an inspiring, galvanizing experience. Surrounded as we are in today's classical music world by hype, by a glorified fixation on the celebrity performer, and by commercial philistinism of all kinds, Seiji Ozawa instead stays true to himself, and true to the original source within himself which made him a musician in the first place.

Seiji is committed to making music in an honest and caring—indeed passionate—way, while always putting the music and the composer first. Rather than using music to project and further himself, Seiji takes a more humble route; he works to make himself a worthy vessel for the music and the composer. He pursues this goal with vigor, discipline, and joy.

I particularly love Seiji's eagerness to keep learning, and the openness that makes this possible. His approach is free of self-satisfaction and altogether free of posturing.

Seiji's love for great music motivates his serious, conscientious study of scores. His consideration of each composition is thorough, probing, and insightful. And having studied with such great care, Seiji can then let go in the playing. It is then not so much a performance as an actual *living* of the music.

Seiji Ozawa's inner fire and intensity bring the music to life. Seiji dances the music, and in that dance he becomes the music.

—PETER SERKIN

Recording session in Symphony Hall with Peter Lieberson (center) and Peter Serkin. Boston, 1984.

With Rudolf Serkin in
Symphony Hall. Boston, 1982.

Recording session for Mahler's Symphony no. 2, with Kiri Te Kanawa, Marilyn Horne, and the BSO. Boston, 1986.

Sitting in the backseat of a Mercedes limousine, speeding through the former East Germany at 2:00 A.M., I could almost make out Seiji Ozawa's expression as he silently and thoughtfully listened to me. He had just completed *Salome* recording sessions with Jessye Norman and the Dresden Staatskapelle Orchestra and was due to begin rehearsals in Berlin at 10:00 the following morning.

I wanted to discuss a few issues with Seiji, someone who could advise me as a professional, an artist, and a colleague, as a friend and a teacher, but who could be as lovingly discreet and as cruelly direct as a member of my own family. I immediately and naturally felt I could turn to Seiji. And though his calendar was, as usual, unbelievably mad, he invited me to join him in Dresden for the final session so that I could meet Miss Norman and his Philips recording crew and so he and I could visit with each other during the four-hour ride to his next stop, Berlin. Sleep?

The content of our discussion was so widely varied as to nearly defy imagination. We spoke of professional topics ranging from discrepancies in a recent Haydn edition to the technique involved in guiding an extremely flexible tempo through a tricky symphonic transition to the choice of soloists for my new recording to sociological and multicultural tensions in the international community as well as in our everyday lives; how these tensions pertained to work attitudes, marriage, family, career priorities; and the possible solutions. I brought these questions to Seiji because I knew that instead of giving me pat answers, he would offer guidance and share his empathy.

We spoke without stopping for the entire trip. Seiji alternated between extreme animation and profound reflection, but throughout he generously offered the unique wisdom of a mature musician who has dared to cross social, economic, and cultural barriers. He also brought to our discussion—as he brings to all his activities—the perspective of one who has achieved inner balance: in his dual roles as mentor and student he has experienced the highest emotional summits and the darkest valleys.

For many years, the extraordinarily talented Seiji Ozawa has established himself and secured a reputation as one of the world's foremost conductors. So much has already been written about him, yet most tributes concentrate on the dazzling aspects of Seiji's genius: his awesome memory, his facility for assimilating scores, and his radical learning curve. But countless musicians whose lives he has touched deeply will always remember him more as a tireless pioneer whose love and devotion to music have made him a great teacher of life. His generosity is overshadowed only by his deference to the greatness of music.

—KENT NAGANO

With Kent Nagano in Peace Park. Hiroshima, 1986.

Ceremonial sake-barrel opening with BSO members Martha Babcock, Malcolm Lowe, and Harry Ellis Dickson. Kofu, 1986.

Backstage in Kanagawa Kenmin Hall talking with
BSO member Michael Zaretsky. Yokohama, 1986.

15

In the Imperial Palace with BSO members (left to right) Ikuko Mizuno and Owen Young, and Her Majesty, Empress Michiko. Tokyo, 1994.

Backstage in the Bunka Kaikan, rehearsing Mahler's Symphony no. 3 with the alto Naoko Ihara, the Kamakura Junior Chorus, and the Shin'yu-kai Chorus. Tokyo, 1986.

With then Crown Prince Akihito and Crown Princess Michiko. Tokyo, 1986.

OZAWA IN PRAYER

When young Seiji Ozawa returned to Japan from France, where he had won acclaim as a gifted conductor, he was interviewed by a host of journalists and myself, then a young writer, equally as young as he. In the interview, Ozawa said that life to him meant realizing music with the whole of his personality. He reiterated tersely and breezily in Japanese, "I music." The media at large quoted this totally new expression and it was soon on the lips of young Japanese.

Nearly forty years have passed since then, and on New Year's Day 1998, on the occasion of a live TV broadcast—a program in which I had the pleasure of conversing with him—he said, "When I'm making music these days, I often feel that I am praying."

Ozawa created beautiful music at the opening ceremony of the Winter Olympics in Nagano. His Beethoven's Ninth Symphony was remarkable. He summoned the world's master musicians to perform in the rural town and, overcoming the time lags of satellite broadcasting, he led six choruses from around the world—South Africa, Australia, Germany, China, and the United States, as well as Japan—in the "Ode to Joy."

Planted in this ceremony was a political intent underscoring the rising tide of Japan's new nationalism. However, against this backdrop, Ozawa daringly joined the Japanese town with diverse areas around the globe and conducted one of the finest musical works of all humankind.

I saw Seiji Ozawa in prayer.

—KENZABURO OE

Laying a wreath in Peace Park.
Hiroshima, 1986.

Conducting in the Herodes Atticus Odeon. Athens, 1994.

Conducting the BSO in the Herodes
Atticus Odeon. Athens, 1991.

Tour-party pyramid: (left to right, bottom) Daniel R. Gustin, Ozawa, Costa Pilavachi, and Josiah Stevenson; (middle) Caroline Smedvig, Martha Batchelor, and Anne Parsons; (top) organist James David Christie and Nancy Knutsen. Kofu, 1986.

Celebrating the BSO's centennial at the Harvard Club with past and present members of the orchestra. Boston, 1981.

27

Backstage in Symphony Hall following the BSO's centennial concert celebration with (left to right) Mstislav Rostropovich, Rudolf Serkin, Leontyne Price, and Isaac Stern. Boston, 1981.

In the Teatro Colón with the late BSO principal clarinetist Harold Wright. Buenos Aires, 1992.

In Symphony Hall with some past and present members of the BSO bass section: (left to right) James Orleans, Robert Olson, John Barwicki, Bela Wurtzler, Lawrence Wolfe, John Salkowski, Joseph Hearne, Edwin Barker, and Leslie Martin. Boston, 1987.

In Symphony Hall with Mstislav Rostropovich. Boston, 1985.

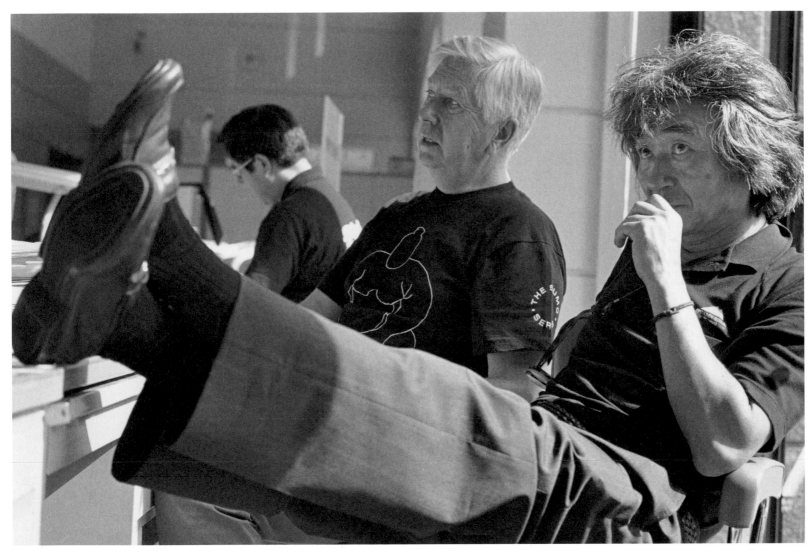

With longtime friend and adviser William Bernell. Matsumoto, 1993.

In the Shed at Tanglewood with BSO timpanist Everett (Vic) Firth. Lenox, 1998.

Whether Seiji is conducting the *Resurrection* Symphony of Mahler or "The Star-Spangled Banner" at a New England Patriots game, he is extremely serious. His dedication and loyalty to his musical craft are unfaltering. The demands he puts on himself, and his expectations of performance from his players, are intense. Every concert is an "event," every rehearsal a "happening." His dedication is unswerving. His musical morals, scruples, principles, and manners are all a part of his dedication. Musicians and nonmusicians alike ask, "What is it like for a player to work with Seiji Ozawa?" First of all, he's a gentleman at all times and fully in control. His methodology is patience, and he rehearses until he achieves his desired musical goals. His stick technique is a player's dream. He's a ballet dancer who possesses a clear, intelligible beat. He has a grace and panache that is unto itself a work of art. He conducts without a score—flawlessly. He never misses a cue, a meter change or any musical subtlety that has been ordained in rehearsal. Perfection and consistency, coupled with his personal élan, are his signature to music.

—VIC FIRTH

In the Shed with Vic Firth and Mark Volpe, BSO managing director. Lenox, 1998.

Backstage in the Grosses Festspielhaus with BSO staff Kim Smedvig and Peter Gelb. Salzburg, 1984.

Backstage in the Nagano-ken Bunka Kaikan with his wife, Vera, and manager Ronald Wilford. Matsumoto, 1993.

Great conductors are rare. A true maestro has to be first of all a dedicated and skilled musician with an aesthetic soul, a leader who can inspire instrumentalists to strive for the interpretation he seeks, an administrator, a public relations genius, a performer, a personnel manager, and a perfectionist. Anyone who embodies all these qualities, and has an unnatural reserve of energy and retains enough humility to escape being a tyrant, has what it takes to be a great conductor.

Which brings me to Seiji Ozawa. My personal observation in dealing with him on broadcast features, listening to his recordings, watching him conduct, is that he scores very high. He garners respect without ever demanding it, his fidelity to a composer's intentions is of the highest order, and his expenditure of personal energy is legendary.

He once complimented me for remembering a sequence of interview questions, which seemed to him noteworthy. I'm sure he was sincere, but I found it curious when within a week I watched him conduct a semistaged production of Strauss's *Elektra* without a score. For an hour and a quarter, he cued every entrance and nuance, had every note in his head! The fact that he admired anyone else's memory struck me as ironic.

His quarter century with the BSO has enriched us all.

—HUGH DOWNS

En route to a tango bar. Buenos Aires, 1992.

Conducting in the Alte Oper.
Frankfurt, 1991.

41

With Japan manager Masa Kajimoto and an unidentified apprentice geisha. Kyoto, 1986.

In Symphony Hall with Kathleen Battle. Boston, 1986.

Curtain call in Symphony Hall with Mstislav Rostropovich. Boston, 1985.

My beloved brother, dearest Seijinka,

I congratulate you on twenty-five years of serving the music with one of the greatest orchestras in the world, my dear colleagues from the Boston Symphony. I am particularly happy that you devoted your musical life precisely to that orchestra, the foundation of which was laid down by that great Russian musician Serge Koussevitzky.

The first time we met, if you remember, was in Toronto, where we played the Second Concerto of Shostakovich. When I came back to Moscow, I said to Shostakovich, "Remember that name—Seiji Ozawa. For certain you will hear again about him." From that day on, each time we meet is for me a holiday, to which I look forward from one concert to another.

Shostakovich once told me, "We are all soldiers of music. Among us there are no generals."

You are to all of us an example of true service to music, and continuous perfection. You are one of the best soldiers of music I have ever met in my life. I embrace you and I bow down before you, my dear, irreplaceable friend. Until the end of my life I remain your Slava-san.

With admiration and love,
MSTISLAV ROSTROPOVICH

Backstage in Symphony Hall
with Rostropovich. Boston, 1985.

Pouring a beer. Matsumoto, 1993.

With street vendors in Japantown. São Paulo, 1992.

With (left to right) Barbara Walt Gustin, Dan Gustin, Sherman Walt, Nancy Knutsen, and Malcolm Lowe. Kyoto, 1986.

Sake toast with the late U.S. Ambassador Mike Mansfield. Tokyo, 1986.

With Kinshi Tsuruta, the late biwa virtuoso; Seiji's mother, Sakura Ozawa; and brother, Mikio (Pon) Ozawa. Matsumoto, 1993.

With Tsuruta and Sakura Ozawa. Matsumoto, 1993.

Curtain-call bouquet in the Bunka Kaikan. Kobe, 1986.

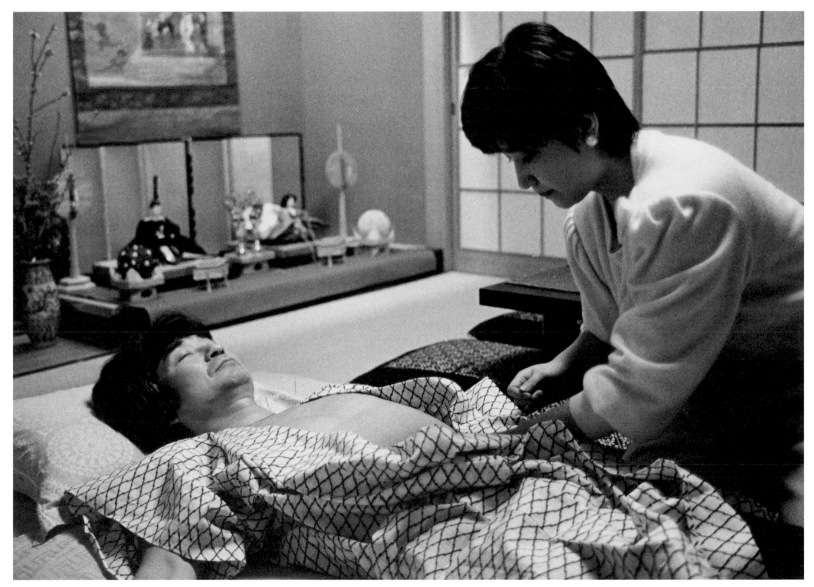

With Noriko Nagato, his acupuncturist. Osaka, 1986.

Rehearsing in Suntory Hall with Peter Serkin. Tokyo, 1995.

With his daughter, Seira. Munich, 1991.

Conducting the BSO in the Alte Oper, with BSO concertmaster Malcolm Lowe. Frankfurt, 1991.

Curtain call in Hitomi Memorial Hall with Malcolm Lowe, Max Hobart, and Marylou Speaker Churchill. Tokyo, 1986.

Overleaf: Rehearsing in the Alte Oper with Jessye Norman and the BSO. Frankfurt, 1991.

Curtain call in the Alte Oper with Jessye Norman. Frankfurt, 1991.

The pleasure of working with Seiji Ozawa is enormous. He is a noble musician who reflects a soul of honor and dignity. Two decades of music-making have given us a special rapport and musical shorthand that is satisfying and comfortable. We enjoy explorations and discoveries together in a wide-ranging repertoire of Mahler, Bizet, Stravinsky, Berg, Ravel, Berlioz, Strauss, and others. Can such a serious musician be fun? An emphatic yes is my reply. Seiji's joy of life is contagious. I look forward to our next voyage.

—JESSYE NORMAN

Backstage in Symphony Hall with John Williams. Boston, 1998.

Backstage in the Shed at Tanglewood with Lauren Bacall. Lenox, 1988.

With BSO players Aza Raykhtsaum, Jules Eskin, Mstislav Rostropovich, and an Erato record executive. Boston, 1985.

Backstage in Smetana Hall with Itzhak Perlman and Yo-Yo Ma. Prague, 1993.

Curtain call in the Philharmonie with Yo-Yo Ma. Berlin, 1984.

Dear Seiji,

Music is the glue that connects many parallel universes that run through your life. I am amazed at how often you can find grace and simplicity in this complex world. Through your talent, perseverance, and faith in the power of music, you have blazed a path for aspiring musicians from all over the globe. The canvas on which you have painted your musical portrait is not yet finished, and we, the listening public and your fellow musicians, are eager to see and hear what is yet to come.

—YO-YO MA

Backstage in the Yamanashi Kenmin Bunka Kaikan with Martha Batchelor. Kofu, 1986.

Backstage at the Gasteig Cultural Center. Munich, 1993.

Overleaf: Tanglewood. Lenox, 1978.

Bravo, Seiji, and congratulations on this twenty-fifth anniversary celebration of your leadership of the Boston Symphony Orchestra! Of course, our happy working collaboration dates back to 1965 at Ravinia and then to appearances in San Francisco, Boston, New York, Tokyo, and elsewhere. You were and are among the most supportive and thoughtful conductors that one could hope for. Not only do you listen to your soloist, but you have an uncanny sense of anticipation, which allows the soloist to be spontaneous and never to have to worry about the orchestra's participation in a given musical moment. You make a concerted musical effort an exciting event. It should always be thus!

To play at Symphony Hall in Boston with the BSO is a wonderful time for any performer. For the leading musical performers, many venues offer success and even occasional pleasure. But very few offer the sense of being embraced—by a hall, by the orchestra, and by the audience—that Symphony Hall does. It will always be a most special place, for those who share a passion for music, to share that passion with fellow musicians and to convey that passion to an attentive and understanding audience.

Tanglewood is one of the icons of summer music festivals, a center to which audiences from all over the country flock and musicians from all over the world come to play and to teach. I remember so many opening nights that we have shared there, including a performance of the Beethoven Concerto when you promised me a beautiful evening and the thunder and the rain practically drowned us out from the beginning of the second movement. Even that has not dampened my enthusiasm, my affection, and my respect for you, for the BSO, and for Tanglewood.

—ISAAC STERN

In Charles Joseph's balloon with his daughter,
Seira, and son, Yuki, at Tanglewood. Lenox, 1984.

Backstage in the Shed at Tanglewood with Leonard Bernstein. Lenox, 1988.

My siblings and I met Seiji in the early sixties, when he was our father's assistant conductor at the New York Philharmonic. Seiji was practically a kid! He was very affectionate with us, full of hugs and smiles. One time his mother came to the States and brought us all beautiful kimonos, altering them right there in our library with her needle and thread. Seiji must not have had a full command of English back then, but I have no memory of that getting in the way of our good times. He was our exotic cousin from the Far East.

We grew up; Seiji grew up. But we all still feel like cousins. It's great having Seiji at Tanglewood in the summers: it keeps everything in the family!

— JAMIE BERNSTEIN

In the Shed at Tanglewood with Leonard Bernstein
and the BSO. Lenox, 1988.

At Seranak with Jack Fitzpatrick and Yo-Yo Ma. Lenox, 1993.

At Seranak with Kent Nagano. Lenox, 1985.

Seiji Ozawa is unlike anyone I've ever met. Classical music is new to me, and it took me awhile to realize how unique Seiji is. His talent is at once sophisticated and primal. He doesn't represent music or interpret it—he is it. To see him conduct is to see a man possessed by music, direct and undiluted. A worldbeater, always in motion, he's at home in Boston or Budapest or Athens, where these pictures of us were taken. Later that same evening we watched him conduct Mahler's Sixth, from memory. Backstage afterward, in his *yukata,* drenched, he receives an old friend. She compliments his dancing. More than any dancer, he makes me see music.

—JAMES TAYLOR

With James Taylor in the
Piraeus district. Athens, 1998.

With his daughter, Seira, and his wife, Vera. Matsumoto, 1993.

With Karen Leopardi and Cleve Morrison. Boston, 1987.

Tour party with then Massachusetts Senate President William Bulger. Munich, 1984.

Seiji's passion for music is universally known. But there is much more to his great enthusiasm for life. I first saw it when he accompanied a group of us to a beer garden in Munich after a strenuous concert. There was a crush of people, strolling musicians with fiddles, tubas, and accordions. The audience began to sing immediately, and carried on throughout the evening. And who set the pace? The maestro himself, loving all the happy fun of this great party. We kept the musicians up late, but they earned every bit of overtime. I love the person who can endure, and on that evening I knew that I had discovered one more reason to appreciate Seiji. His passion for music and life cheers the hearts of all who are privileged to know him.

—WILLIAM M. BULGER

With Blanca del Rey. Madrid, 1991.

I was asked to join in the special twenty-fifth anniversary tribute to Seiji Ozawa because over the past four years I have had the unique experience of both watching the maestro conduct the Boston Symphony Orchestra and attending New England Patriots games with him. Seiji exudes the same excitement, enthusiasm, and passion in the concert hall and in the stands. During a game, he constantly asks me questions that reveal his curious mind. He understands the necessary talent, artistry, and team effort required for perfect execution — not unlike the requirements for an orchestra to perform at its highest level. Leadership and teamwork are vital for special results in football *and* music, and Seiji is one of those rare individuals who can cross cultural lines and understand both.

It is rare to find an icon of art who is so at home in the arena of sports. In Boston we have been fortunate to have had Seiji for twenty-five years as the music director of the Boston Symphony Orchestra, and the New England Patriots have been lucky to have Seiji as their number-one fan. Each time Seiji has conducted the national anthem at a Patriots game, we have won. With his help, we hope to play in the Super Bowl and win again.

—ROBERT K. KRAFT

Playing tennis. Tokyo, 1986.

In an *onsen*. Matsumoto, 1993.

Iguaçu Falls. Brazil, 1992.

Called back onstage by an
enthusiastic audience. Osaka, 1994.

"Only German conductors understand Brahms."

"A conductor has to be Italian to do justice to Verdi."

"Ah, the Russians! They really know their way

around Tchaikovsky!"

Such statements are favorites of a postconcert crowd. They are good, safe clichés of nationalism, and undoubtedly they sometimes hit the mark. However, none of these generalizations can serve as a hiding place after a concert conducted by Seiji Ozawa.

Seiji is musically at home everywhere. The orchestras of Boston, Vienna, Berlin, Paris, and Tokyo welcome him. If I were to start listing his memorable performances, I would have to include such diverse bedfellows as Mozart's *Idomeneo,* Mahler's Third, Honegger's *Joan of Arc, Tosca,* and the all-time champion, *Rite of Spring,* which is a piece Seiji should take out a personal patent on. His technique is simply flawless and it enables him to be utterly in control at all times. He is certainly the most elegant conductor around, expressive and fluid and wonderfully clear. His memory is enough to turn most of his colleagues an interesting shade of envy green. He led his first *St. Matthew Passion* from memory, and even the premiere of Messiaen's marathon *St. Francis,* a work that might best be timed with a sundial. Seiji takes all this as a matter of course, but without ever seeming facile. He studies endlessly and never takes a performance for granted. A good

Laughing at a joke. Matsumoto, 1993.

Backstage with his Japan managers Motoo Hirasa and Naoyasu Kajimoto. Matsumoto, 1993.

example is the annual traditional playing of the *1812 Overture* at Tanglewood. His rehearsals for this very familiar piece are as detailed and thorough as if a premiere were at stake.

As a human being, Seiji is kind and generous. Generosity toward colleagues is a rare commodity in a profession where *jalousie de métier* is nurtured and honed to perfection. His compliments and gratitude are serious and touching. Two years ago, I helped conduct the triple birthday concert for Seiji, Itzhak Perlman, and Yo-Yo Ma, and at the postperformance party I found myself among a group that included Yo-Yo. Seiji strolled over and grasped me by the hand. "You know, André, I will never forget what you did for us today," he said. He turned to Yo-Yo and asked earnestly, "Don't you agree?" Yo-Yo took my other hand. "I will forget it tomorrow," he said happily. I liked both statements, both typical, both equal expressions of friendship.

Seiji learned long ago that most music criticism is as durable as an autumn leaf and that a lifetime commitment to work is everything. His knowledge of music is encyclopedic. His respect for tradition and scholarliness is deep. But finally, more important than all the attributes that can be gleaned from text is an abiding and faithful love of the music. Seiji proves that over and over again, every time he stands in front of his orchestra, leading it with authority, grace, and affection.

—ANDRÉ PREVIN

Signing autographs backstage in the Grosses Festspielhaus. Salzburg, 1984.

BSO trustees' president Dr. Nicholas T. Zervas and former BSO Managing Director Kenneth Haas offer congratulations at Seiji's sixtieth birthday celebration as Vera Ozawa and Mstislav Rostropovich look on. Tokyo, 1995.

In Symphony Hall, rehearsing
the BSO with Hildegard Behrens
and Nadine Secunde in Strauss's
Elektra. Boston, 1987.

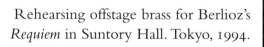

Rehearsing offstage brass for Berlioz's
Requiem in Suntory Hall. Tokyo, 1994.

With his mother Sakura, his daughter Seira, his son Yukiyoshi, his wife Vera, and Vera's mother Kimi Motoki Ilyin. Lenox, 1985.

Down to earth, messy hair, big tennis lover, very, very serious when it comes to music, always apologizing for his poor English when he gives speeches (but his Japanese isn't that rich either . . .), able to concentrate 120 percent whenever wherever he wants to, often has bathroom meetings in his dressing room after concerts, loves to make people laugh at his jokes (this is when his family suffers), wakes up at 4:00 A.M. no matter how tired he is if he needs to memorize more of his scores, cannot resist NBA games on TV, honest-hearted, loves Gap T-shirts, never admits I am taller than he, orders *only* spaghetti vongole and arugula salads at Italian restaurants, always tries to go to Patriots games, a genius at turning a tidy room into a bombed place in less than five minutes . . .

I know all of these sentences will make sense to my dad's friends. (Don't they?)

To me, he is a fun and great papa whom I respect a lot and at the same time, he is my *best* friend ever. I can talk to him about anything and I know he'll understand me. (Sometimes we fight, of course, but I usually win!!!)

When I was to go to elementary school, my parents brought me to my dad's old school in Tokyo. I had a hard time blending in because I was from a foreign country. At the same time, I developed serious asthma from the change of climate.

When I had asthma attacks and had a hard time breathing, Dad called from Boston. I could not really talk because of the attack, so he was the one who did the talking then. He'd apologize for not being with me and would tell me he'd change places with me if he could. Before hanging up the phone, he'd always promise to call the next day and would pray for me, and I knew he had tears in his eyes because his voice was a bit funny and shaky. I still had hard nights when I had the attacks, but I remember I always felt stronger after I talked to him.

What I love about my dad is that he is very honest with himself and therefore with his family and friends. In Boston, he cares very much about his fellow musicians. Boston is his other home besides Tokyo.

My two favorite words in Japanese are *nakama* and *jingi*. *Nakama* are friends and fellows who aim for the same goal and help each other to achieve that goal, and *jingi* is loyalty and honesty and the absence of trickery. I think Dad is a person with *jingi*. I think most of his *nakama* in Boston have the same quality. A place filled with such *nakama* is very rare, and it makes me proud when I am in Boston to feel that I'm a tiny part of it.

—SEIRA OZAWA

With Vera, Seira, and Yuki. Matsumoto, 1993.

In Ozawa Hall at Tanglewood.
Lenox, 1998.

Chronology
Seiji Ozawa and the Boston Symphony Orchestra

1959 After winning first prize at the Besançon International Conducting Competition, Seiji Ozawa is invited by then BSO Music Director Charles Munch to study at Tanglewood. Soon thereafter he hears Munch and the Boston Symphony Orchestra for the first time during the orchestra's first-ever tour to Japan.

1960 Seiji Ozawa arrives at the Berkshire Music Center (now the Tanglewood Music Center), the Boston Symphony's summer training academy in Lenox, Massachusetts, works with Charles Munch and conducting instructor Eleazar de Carvalho; this marks the beginning of his long association with the BSO. At the end of that summer, he is awarded the Koussevitzky Prize for Outstanding Student Conductor.

1964 Ozawa makes his first guest-conducting appearance with the Boston Symphony on August 16 at Tanglewood; the program includes Bizet's Symphony in C, Hindemith's *Mathis der Maler,* and Mussorgsky's *Pictures at an Exhibition.* He makes encore appearances during the 1965, 1966, and 1967 summer seasons.

1968 Seiji Ozawa leads his first BSO concert in Symphony Hall on January 26; the program includes music of Gluck and Joachim, as well as Bernstein's Symphony no. 2, "The Age of Anxiety," and Ravel's second suite from *Daphnis et Chloé.* The following week he brings the same program to Hartford, New York's Philharmonic Hall, and Brooklyn.

1969 As guest conductor, Ozawa makes his first recordings with the Boston Symphony at Symphony Hall—Orff's *Carmina Burana* and Stravinsky's *Petrushka* and the suite from *The Firebird*—for the RCA Victor label.

1970 Seiji Ozawa is appointed an artistic adviser for the BSO at Tanglewood, along with Gunther Schuller as head of the Tanglewood Music Center and Leonard Bernstein as general adviser.

1972 In February, Ozawa is appointed music adviser for the Boston Symphony Orchestra's 1972–73 season and music director starting with the 1973–74 season.

1973 At age thirty-eight, Seiji Ozawa conducts his first program as the thirteenth music director of the Boston Symphony Orchestra, Berlioz's *Damnation of Faust* on September 28, and leads the BSO in the same piece two weeks later for his Carnegie Hall debut. The BSO performs the work for Deutsche Grammophon, marking the first recording for Ozawa as music director, resulting in his first Grammy nomination.

1974 *Evening at Symphony,* the orchestra's televised concert series, produced by WGBH-TV for national broadcast on PBS, is launched. The series earns Seiji Ozawa an Emmy for Outstanding Achievement in Musical Direction in 1976.

1975 Seiji Ozawa makes his first American tour with the BSO, performing in Detroit; Ann Arbor; Indianapolis; Bloomington, Indiana; Chicago; Wheaton, Illinois; and Iowa City.

1976 Ozawa makes his first international tour with the BSO, playing to audiences in Amsterdam, Brussels, Vienna, Linz, Munich, Berlin, Hamburg, London, Bonn, Hannover, and Paris.

1977 Ozawa and the BSO's recording of Berlioz's *Romeo and Juliet* on Deutsche Grammophon is awarded the Grand Prix du Disque.

1978 Seiji Ozawa and the BSO travel to Japan for the first time together, with concerts in Fukuoka, Kokura, Hiroshima, Osaka, Kyoto, Anazawa, Nagoya, Yokohama, and Tokyo. It is the BSO's second tour to Japan, the first having been led by Charles Munch in 1960.

1979 Seiji Ozawa and the Boston Symphony make history as the first Western orchestra to perform in mainland China following the establishment of diplomatic relations with the United States. Concerts, coachings, and master classes are given in Shanghai and Beijing.

1980 *The Boston Goes to China,* the CBS documentary about the BSO's historic visit to China, is awarded four Emmys, for Best Documentary, Best Direction, Best Editing, and Best Sound.

Seiji Ozawa leads a performance of Puccini's *Tosca* at Tanglewood, initiating a series of semistaged operas under his direction at Tanglewood and in Symphony Hall, which will continue with performances of Puccini's *Madama Butterfly* during his twenty-fifth anniversary season at Symphony Hall.

1981 Seiji Ozawa and the BSO celebrate the orchestra's centennial with a gala concert on October 18 featuring the violinists Itzhak Perlman and Isaac Stern, the soprano Leontyne Price, the cellist Mstislav Rostropovich, and the pianist Rudolf Serkin; a free Hundredth Birthday Concert featuring Beethoven's Ninth Symphony is performed on Boston Common on October 22. The year also includes two centennial tours, across the United States in March and to Japan and Europe in October and November.

In all, twelve works are commissioned for the orchestra's centennial, including works for the BSO, the Boston Pops, the Boston Symphony Chamber Players, and the Tanglewood Festival Chorus. World premieres of a number of these works are given during this season, including Leonard Bernstein's Divertimento for Orchestra (1980), Peter Maxwell Davies's Symphony no. 2, and Roger Sessions's Concerto for Orchestra, which earns Sessions the 1982 Pulitzer Prize in Musical Composition.

1982 A recording of Beethoven's *Emperor* Concerto with Rudolf Serkin and the BSO led by Seiji Ozawa is released on the Telarc label, inaugurating their cycle of the composer's piano concertos.

1983 Seiji Ozawa and the BSO celebrate ten years together with a tour of the United States, including performances in Cleveland, Ann Arbor, Columbus, Cincinnati, and Lexington, Kentucky.

1984 Ozawa and the BSO perform their first concert staging in Symphony Hall: Arthur Honegger's dramatic oratorio *Jeanne d'Arc au Bûcher*. The following week, the same production is given at Carnegie Hall; the *New York Times* names it one of the best musical events of the year.

1985 Ozawa's fiftieth birthday is marked at Tanglewood on September 1 with a special guest, Itzhak Perlman, who celebrated his fortieth one day earlier, in an all-Beethoven concert drawing an audience of 17,734, a record at that time.

1986 Seiji Ozawa leads the BSO in the American premiere of three scenes from Olivier Messiaen's monumental opera *St. Francis of Assisi* in Boston, followed by performances in New York's Carnegie Hall. The bass-baritone José van Dam, the tenor Kenneth Riegel, and the soprano Kathleen Battle are soloists, with the Tanglewood Festival Chorus and John Oliver, conductor.

1987 Seiji Ozawa and the BSO present acclaimed performances of Strauss's *Elektra,* with Hildegard Behrens in the title role and Christa Ludwig as Clytemnestra. The production is repeated the following year and recorded by Philips, marking Seiji Ozawa's first opera recording with the BSO.

Ozawa, the highly acclaimed 1985 documentary by the leading American filmmakers Albert and David Maysles, airs on PBS's *Great Performances* and is subsequently released on home video.

1988 Seiji Ozawa and the BSO participate in a gala, star-studded performance at Tanglewood celebrating Leonard Bernstein's seventieth birthday, on August 25. *Bernstein at 70!* is broadcast on PBS's *Great Performances* the following March and wins an Emmy for Outstanding Classical Program in the Performing Arts.

1989 Ozawa appoints a player to the BSO for the fiftieth time; more than 70 percent of the current orchestra is composed of musicians whom he has chosen.

1990 Seiji Ozawa and the BSO's recording of Strauss's *Elektra* is nominated for a Grammy Award and named a Record of the Year by *Stereo Review.*

1991 The BSO's first video laser disk is released on the Sony Classical label, with Seiji Ozawa leading the orchestra in Brahms's Symphony no. 1 and Strauss's *Also Sprach Zarathustra.* The performance was recorded during the orchestra's 1986 Japan tour.

Ozawa leads the thousandth BSO concert at Tanglewood, on August 16.

Ozawa and the BSO perform concert stagings of Tchaikovsky's *Pique Dame* with the soprano Mirella Freni, the tenor Vladimir Atlantov, and the baritone Dmitri Hvorostovsky in Symphony Hall. The performances are recorded live for RCA Victor, marking a renewed collaboration with this label. The recording is nominated for a Grammy for Best Opera Recording in 1993.

1992   Seiji Ozawa leads the BSO on its first tour to South America, performing in São Paulo, Buenos Aires, and Caracas.

Ozawa conducts his thousandth concert during the 1991–92 Symphony Hall subscription season. To date, he has led nearly 1,400 concerts with the orchestra in Symphony Hall, at Tanglewood, and throughout the world.

1993   Seiji Ozawa and the BSO celebrate twenty years together with a special opening-night all-Berlioz program featuring the soprano Sylvia McNair, the mezzo-soprano Frederica von Stade, the tenor Jerry Hadley, and the baritone Benjamin Luxon. The season also includes a European tour with performances in London, Paris, Madrid, Vienna, Milan, Munich, and Prague.

This year also marks the world premiere of Hans Werner Henze's Symphony no. 8, commissioned by Seiji Ozawa and the BSO.

1994   Seiji Ozawa receives his second Emmy Award, for Individual Achievement in Cultural Programming, for the PBS telecast *Dvořák in Prague: A Celebration,* a program produced in 1993 during that season's European tour.

A new era begins for the Tanglewood Music Center with the opening of Seiji Ozawa Hall and the Leonard Bernstein Campus.

1995   Seiji Ozawa and the BSO's recording of Mahler's Third and Sixth symphonies is released, completing the full cycle of Mahler symphonies on the Philips label.

Ozawa and the BSO's recording of Bartók's Concerto for Orchestra, incorporating the composer's original ending, is released on the Philips label to mark the fiftieth anniversary of the premiere of this important BSO commission.

Seiji Ozawa, Itzhak Perlman, and Yo-Yo Ma celebrate their sixtieth, fiftieth, and fortieth birthdays, respectively, at a gala concert at Tanglewood entitled "The Three Birthdays," drawing an audience of 18,709.

Ozawa and the BSO give the American premiere of Sir Michael Tippett's *The Rose Lake,* a commission that would be Sir Michael's final work.

1996   Seiji Ozawa and the BSO perform the world premiere of George Walker's *Lilacs,* a work commissioned by the BSO for a special tribute to the late African-American tenor Roland Hayes; Walker is awarded the Pulitzer Prize for Music Composition for his work.

1997   Seiji Ozawa and the BSO give the world premiere of Henri Dutilleux's *The Shadows of Time,* a work that they commissioned. The piece is to be recorded by Erato in March 1998 for release in Europe when the BSO gives the French premiere in Paris the following week, while the orchestra is on tour in Europe.

Plans are announced for the opening ceremonies of the 1998 Winter Olympics at Nagano, Japan. Seiji Ozawa is to lead the finale of Beethoven's Ninth Symphony with an orchestra composed of members from around the world, including four BSO players, and five choruses on five continents, including the Tanglewood Festival Chorus representing the Western Hemisphere, all linked by satellite to the Olympic stadium in Nagano.

1998   With the opening-night concert on September 23, Seiji Ozawa will surpass Serge Koussevitzky's twenty-five-year tenure with the BSO. Koussevitzky led his first concert as music director on October 10, 1924, and his final one on August 14, 1949, at Tanglewood.

Seiji Ozawa and the BSO celebrate twenty-five years together with a special Silver Anniversary Season in 1998–99, including a free performance on the Boston Common of Beethoven's Ninth Symphony, a concert staging of Puccini's *Madama Butterfly,* and a tour to China and Japan.